Down the Trails of Life

Lord Lead the Way

Milton Bullard Jr.

Down the Trails of Life: Lord Lead the Way

Published by TaylorMade Publishing
Jacksonville, FL
www.TaylorMadePublishingFL.com
(904) 323-1334

TaylorMade Publishing

Table of Contents

Introduction i

Budding Tree 1

Beyond the "Veil" 2

The Pierced Darkness 4

The Journey Home...5

Under God's Tree of Love 6

Face to Face with God 7

The Crossroad...9

Entering into His Glory 10

God Cares 11

Still...12

When the dust settles 13

The Greatest Call of Love...15

"Beulah Land" 17

Paid in Full 19

In You, O God..20

He Came to Be 22

Strength in Weakness..24

Those Moments...25

About the Author 26

Introduction

Authenticity is a rare quality to find in today's modern age. The art of face-to-face communication and personal interactions have slipped away into the vast digital era. The technology we have deemed so dear and vital to make the world better has resulted in a world in which we "merely exist," but do not truly live. The ability to touch lives through sincere, meaningful dialogue is slowly disappearing, possibly to never return. The sharing of ideas or personal challenges, whether good or bad, is now seldom expressed by a smile, grin, tears, or glimmer in the eyes of people as they voice their deepest concerns, joys, or trials.

My hope is that you will find on these pages the God who is real, personable, and genuinely cares. He is a God who listens to the smallest details of our unspoken cries in the dry, desolate places of our hearts, minds, and lives. Places where no one is allowed nor would dare to enter. But God can. God listens to our most earnest prayers, never forgets and answers in His timely manner.

I pray God will place an everlasting hope, strength, and assurance in your heart as you read these pages. Whatever and wherever that hilltop or deep, dark valley in life has brought you to, be assured of this, God is there to be the Lord of your life, for He cares for you.

Budding Tree

A budding tree
Young, alive, strong, and free
Its arms are reaching out,
Without a reason why
To touch a moon, cloud, star, or sky.

Its legs are strong and firm,
Without a curl
To withstand the evil
In this ever-changing wicked world.

Don't water it with lies,
hatred nor deceit,
It kills its roots, destroy its fruits, stunts its growth
Aiding in its defeat.

The Great Son of heaven, Master of Assemblies
That reigns, rules, and resides above
Is watering and filling it with
His power, strength, wisdom, and love.

Give it water, make it strong
For all to see
Because that budding bush
Could be him, her, you, or me.

Beyond the "Veil"

Egypt's taskmasters hated the children of God
Treated them like they were a slave
They were bruised, beaten, and worked tirelessly
Yet, only to Almighty God, praises they gave.

The newborn baby boys
Scheduled for death the moment born
Revealed Pharoah's hatred for the soon coming King
His devious plot revealed his scorn.

As Pharoah plotted and boiled
In his sin, hatred, and anger
Only Almighty God knew peace and deliverance
Would arrive from His Son, born in a manger.

So, they ate their food in fear and tears by Egypt's fleshpots of bondage
And the Lord heard their heart-wrenching wail
Yet, it just was not the perfect time
For God did not let them see beyond the veil.

Then, came all the plagues of Egypt
They were relentless and without fail
The children of Israel moved swiftly
Yet, numb to their deliverance hanging beyond the veil.

The great waters stood on ends and were divided
As they blazed across the dry land trail
Yet, they still could not know nor see
What rest beyond the veil.

There was such a great multitude
Walking across the "dry" sea floor
Moving with such haste after being
Delivered by the Lamb's blood above each door.

In the wilderness, their eyes and hearts would wax cold
Grumbling at Moses and Aaron, they would assail
Yet, God would only allow some a glimpse
Of the majesty hidden beyond the veil.

[2]

Generations passed and time went on
As the Bible would tell
Yet, God controls everything even the time
He would reveal the One hidden beyond the veil.

On that long, dusty road to Damascus
Paul trembling, eyes covered with scales
No food, no water and dark were his days
God restored his vision, allowing him to peer beyond the veil.

He saw the Risen, Great Savior, Prince of Peace
As the prophets of old did foretell
Given only to those who would just simply believe
Only they would be able to see the blessings beyond the veil.

That veil was rent from top to bottom
Proclaiming only Jesus defeated the grave, death, and hell
Making salvation open only to those who
Would simply believe and repent so they could enter through the veil.

The Pierced Darkness

There are places we run to
Where wickedness and evil hide
Those places of shame and guilt
Where no light or truth abide.

Places of sin, death, and torment
That keeps our tortured souls torn asunder
Shackling our hearts, our minds
Making us doubt and wonder.

But as the light of the Gospel of Jesus
Shines and breaks the darkness apart
We know it will continuously permeate
The deep, dark trenches of our heart.

Satan has erected walls
To keep us bound within
But God has sent His only begotten Son
To set at liberty those shackled in sin.

He is our peace and overseer
The anchor of our soul
The Captain of our salvation
There, in Him alone, we have been made whole.

God is our mighty fortress
Standing as a strong tower
To release His Holy Spirit
As proof of His everlasting power.

The Journey Home

As I look toward the future
There are so many things I expect.
As I drift through this life reminiscing the past
There are many things I regret.

But God has brought me on
This long journey to and fro
I dare not think; not for one moment
He is ready to let me go.

He has carried me over the steepest hills of life
The lowest valleys too,
The brightest, joyous days
Always kissed me with His morning dew.

He has knocked down many walls
No one could ever climb
He has built a fortress around me
To protect me all the time.

He has brightened my every step
During the darkened day
Lost, confused, lonely
When no one would come my way.

Now I think it is over
Because my earthly chore is done
God will fold His loving arms around me
To say, "A job well done, my Son."

These are the words to hear
That have been my life-long quest
To hear my Savior say
"Come enter into my rest."

Under God's Tree of Love

Under God's tree of love
I meditate on His Word
Under God's tree of love
The things of this world grow ever so absurd.

Yet, under God's tree of love, His Word makes life so clear
Sound as a bell,
Cleansing my soul, purging my sins,
Driving me far from destruction and hell.

Your Living Word came from heaven above
Making my heart sing,
and soul laugh
Under God's tree of love.

There is a song my heart is singing
The words I know quite so well
Words of joy, love, and peace
Thoughts deeper than the deepest well.

Words that bring so much joy
My soul explodes within
Words of love wider than the universe
Compassion, patience my earthly mind cannot comprehend.

Face to Face with God

Please do not stand crying over me
Do not sigh or moan
All you see is a lifeless corpse in a deep, dark hole
For my dear friend, I am gone.

I have been lifted above the eagle's nest, cloud's domain
Far, far above the human race
Only to set my longing gaze
Upon my Savior's face.

A face that beholds
No mistakes, sins, or blame
A face that has blotted out
All my transgressions, guilt, and shame.

A face that puts my wretched mind
Into a heavenly state of rest
Casting the scourge of my soul
As far as east is from west.

A face that knows no sorrow
And holds no tears
A loving face
That has covered and erased all my fears.

Haunting fears: full of disappointments and disgust
Leaving me standing all alone
Gripping fears of judgement, punishment, and eternal damnation
Due payment for the wicked, corrupt seeds I have sown.

Seeds of lies, division, hatred
That have torn me apart
Planted and watered by that Old Deceiver
Cursing my dark soul and heart.

Eyes that reflect no vision
Of the wrongful deeds I have done
All my sins are covered, buried under the cleansing
Blood of God's Only begotten Son.

A smile that brings this vile man
Bent to his knees
Weeping in godly sorrow for the undeserved forgiveness
And eternal love I received.

A love that showered me directly
From the Great I AM
Eternally washing, purging my sins
By the blood of the Risen Lamb.

The Crossroad

I came to this Crossroad
For my life was covered with sinful dross
Yet, I was amazed by its wonderful, cleansing light
That made me realize I was hopelessly lost.

There, alone I stood
Filled with guilt and shame
No family, friend or even foe stood by me
For I was the one to blame.

I saw my sins burdening me
Even from the day of my birth
All the good I had done
There, as I stood, it was of no value or worth.

A still, small voice echoed beyond this amazing Cross
"Why do you stand bewildered and grieve?
Call on my name, confess your sins
Repent and just simply believe."

Believe I AM HE
Of whom the prophets of old foretold
Who came and did all said,
In the days of old.

Believe I AM the Burden Bearer,
Bread of Life and Forgiver of sins,
Believe I AM the Only One that could bring to naught
The eternal destruction of men.

As the fig tree is Israel
A growing bud
Believe I AM that I AM
He that gives life through His blood.

The burden was lifted, heart enlightened
From what I heard
Hope came alive and my life was filled with a purpose
Because of God's Living and Spoken Word.

Entering into His Glory

When I was a young lad of seven or eight
And heard the salvation story
I was so excited and impressed
Of one day entering into His glory.

His death was cruel and horrible
In the plan of His-Story
But He went through it all without sin
So I could enter into His glory.

What an awful way to die
Stretched out on Calvary's Cross
Between the earth and the sky.

His death was a shame and yet so gory
But He faced it all
So, believers could enter into His glory.

Now many will hear the message
Telling the age-old salvation story
But those who will not commit to Him
Will not enter into His glory.

Now, I am an old man
And have never regretted hearing the salvation story
Yet, I am overwhelmed inside at the thought
Of one day seeing His face when I enter into His glory.

God Cares

Life is a strange tragedy
Yet, a serious comedy at its best
Those winding roads, dark valleys, and hilltops
Springing up but never giving us a moments rest.

Almighty God has a hand in this
He has planned it that way
So, in the daily trials of living
He asks us to call on Him day by day.

Not a moment given where we should ever think
We can stand on our own.
Yet, in His strength, in His power
There, in His presence, only then, can we carry on.

This maddening race at such an exhausting pace
To reach only God knows where
All our troubles, trials, and challenges on His shoulder
He is more than able to bear.

He bears the pain of our past, present and future too
Afflictions: we alone, without a doubt, could never carry
If left on our own and all alone
We, they would surely bury.

Us under such an insurmountable weight
That shatters our earthly goals
Killing our weakened spirit
Crushing our weary-ridden souls.

So, cast all your cares and daily worries upon Him
For He is faithful and true
You will surely find, far more than one time
That He cares for you.

Still

I can see Him coming
He seems much closer than afar
My eyes can dimly see Him, but
My heart and soul know exactly who they are.

I see Him on the horizon
His urgent coming will be without delay
I must be covered, clothed and ready
His presence, power, truth, and righteousness will be on display.

He comes with glad tidings
His promises to fulfill
I have been waiting, patiently, expectantly
Ever so poised for Him to still.

Still the rush of an evil-menacing world
With all its evil intentions
To destroy my peace, love, and faith
While battling for all my attention.

Still the devourer's crafty onslaught
His destructive, divisive, wicked ways
Leading many into darkness and death
Stealing the promises of their eternal days.

Those days of eternal peace, power
And of His presence they will sing
His truth, righteousness while
Ruling as God's only heavenly King.

Beautiful melodies will be voiced
All across heaven's domain
Triumphant words of victory, joy, and gladness
The darkness of this world will never refrain.

When The Dust Settles

When the dust settles
My hearing will be ever so clear.
When the dust settles
I can see afar; I can see near.

When the dust settles and I
Look down over my life from heaven above
I pray not to be found lacking
In showing others God's great love.

His great love through kindness
That stripped me of my pride
As I took pleasure in His glorious light
Where sin, wickedness, and darkness can never abide.

His great gift of forgiveness
Made me wonder, How can this be?
That unshackled my corrupt, stubborn soul
Setting me eternally free.

His only way of salvation
Purchased at such a great cost
Paid with the precious blood of Jesus
Once and for all on Calvary's Cross.

His great love and power
To battle the without and within
Those evil forces that kept me bound
In the trenches or abyss that I could never win.

It was just simply God's great love
So complete yet mere mortal words cannot explain
Flooding my soul day after day
With such power the universe cannot restrain.

A love that will show
My heart was not blind
To the toils, trials, and
Many sufferings of mankind.

Did my hands reach out
Or feet swiftly run to help
When I saw others stumble or trip
Or did I fail to notice the halt in their step?

Did I offer my food or water
To relieve their strain
When I saw their bodies aching or writhing
Or faces grimace while in pain.

Did I try to wipe it with a smile
The many tears that streamed down their saddened face
Or did I try to put laughter in their burdened hearts
As I was moved only by God's amazing grace.

So, when the dust settles
Did I let His great love flow in
To fill my soul so I can give it out
Only to be eternally filled again.

The Greatest Call of Love

Down through the stretches of time
A Call was voiced into the darkness of sin
As they trembled in guilt, shame, and blame
It is here where the Call had to begin.

This Call came walking in the cool of day saying
"Where art thou? a voice they once loved to hear
But now in their darkness, shivering in their sin
They hid in shame and fear.

Fear of the unknown and to their surprise
Living in an evil, wicked and dark existence
That old serpent had destroyed their Paradise
They ate sin's bitter fruit void of God's goodness and radiance.

The bitter taste of sin
Enveloped their hearts, minds, and soul
Left them groping in the darkness
Blindly standing at the edge of a great threshold.

That great threshold marked the fruit of their disobedience
Which would punish, haunt mankind through the ages
But God had warned them before their transgression
As outlined upon His loving, inspiring pages.

Only because of God's great love
He had to make this urgent Call
To as many who would answer and believe in Him
He would save after such a great fall.

A fall that had the parents of mankind
Hiding, scared among the Garden of Eden's trees
While Satan scorned, laughed, and tricked them
Because they doubted and disobeyed God's decree.

They stood bewildered in their darkness
A place they now possessed but had never known
God's peace and the beauty of His glorious paradise
Was suddenly interrupted, marred, suddenly gone.

[15]

Guilt tore at their hearts, piercing their souls asunder
While shame was written across their face
This was such an unfamiliar territory
They once lived in innocence, flooded with God's love and grace.

Paradise that was always full of good
A solitude that gave them God's perfect rest
Now wickedness, darkness had fallen, night had come
Fear tore at their souls while their hearts pounded within their chests.

Now they saw their nakedness
A most painful, cruel sight to see
Their evil intentions surfaced and shifted
Blaming all within sight for their sad, sinful misery.

In a frantic haste, in great fear
They sewed fig leaves together to cover the deed done
God would first shed blood to cover them
Foreshadowing the work of His only begotten Son.

The deceiver, old serpent had made his mark
His curse would be felt down through the ages
Yet, God already had the cure for the curse of mankind
Words fingered on His loving pages.

The old serpent would bruise the Savior's heel
In the place He would tread
But our Savior would destroy this plague of mankind
By crushing the serpent's head.

Without the love and grace of God
All would be eternally lost
Satan could boast and win
But all of mankind would pay a dreadful cost.

So, when you go to your knees to pray
Thanking God for His blessing that came down from above
Let His Word be written upon your hearts
As you thank Him for His Greatest Call of Love.

"Beulah Land"

I see this beautiful land
It is not too far away
Time is steadily passing by
It shall overtake us one day.

I see a beautiful land
The righteous walk upright for they are wise
Liars, deceivers, and haters of God
This country will be their demise.

A land where children laugh and sing
Songs of the goodness of God
A land where evil, death, and wickedness
Will never be able to trod.

A land where faces have no tears
And griefs, conflicts are never seen
A place where the hearts of mankind
Are full of God's love, grace, pure and clean.

A land where the Spirit of God
Remains forever to fill the entire space
A country created by the Lord
For all the human race.

For the former things are dissolved
Never to return and have passed away
The Sovereign God of the universe
Only His power, His majesty will be on display.

A land filled with Gods' goodness, where
Truth, peace, and righteousness reign
Evil, wickedness, and hatred
There, it will never be sustained.

For the Master of Assemblies
Has flooded hearts with His eternal love
His mercy, grace, salvation, and power
Will be their life's blood.

A land that is not made
By the works, wit, or hand of man
A perfect dwelling place,
Our final resting space
Called by God, "Beulah Land".

Paid in Full

One day, these gray hairs will not be seen in disgust
Because when I look up to You
In Ye, and Ye alone, O Lord
Do I put all my trust.

My crooked, imperfect teeth
Been there for a while
No matter the dental work
They still cramp my style.

The many wrinkled lines on my face
Give away my age
Yet, my name is written in the Lamb's Book of life
Fingered by God on every page.

My eyes always start to gleam
Every time my heart and soul fall in place
Knowing that I am washed in your forgiveness
Your, love, mercy, and matchless grace.

So, you see I have been purchased with a price
And cannot be bought no more
So, this land can keep its earthly gifts
That comes from its worldly store.

My treasures are stored in heaven above
They have been tried, tested and true
They have been purchased with the precious blood of the lamb
Unto Him, my allegiance due.

In You, O God

A man labors throughout his troubled days
To get and store up all he can make
Never realizing when his life is over
Nothing with him, will he take.

His children, wife is just on loan
And not his to own nor possess
But they are thine, O God
And thine alone; he must surely confess.

He does not know where
To turn nor what to do
Yet, dear Lord hopefully he will see
He is eternally lost without you.

So, where is he to go and what is he to do
Just look unto the Lord
Believe in Him
Search to find where God has planted His truth.

The answer is sketched on the pages of your Holy Writ
All to be fulfilled and never to depart
But in you, O God, want them written
Upon the tables of his heart.

It is in you, O God that
Brought him out of the dread and darkness of life
Disguised as good but filled with
All sorts of trouble, confusion, deceit, and strife.

The gentle whispers of your commandments
Guided him day by day
Talking, comforting, and moving him
To walk in love and humility along this Christian way.

It is in you, O God that
The sun lights upon and warms his face
Making him so thankful for your everlasting
Salvation and matchless grace.

It is in you, O God
That he finds this race of life is won
Not by possessions, wealth, or fame
But by the finished works of your only begotten Son.

He Came to Be

He came to be for me what
I could never be for myself
He came alone
And did it all by Himself.

He came to be my Peace
In a world of sin and despair
A world ruled by evil and wickedness
Running rampant, abiding everywhere.

He came to be my Provider
When no one could meet my needs
No matter how much I begged
Only He heard and answered all my pleads.

My provider came when I
Was destitute, hungry, thirsty and in despair
My fresh manna that fell daily
Provided more than enough for me, now I can share.

He came to be my Protector
When trouble compassed me all about
When the afflictions of my soul
Surrounded me within and without.

He came to be my Savior
When all was lost
There was nothing I could do
For me, He paid the ultimate cost.

He came to be for me
What I could never be
That Lamb of God, Perfect Sacrifice
That willingly came, gave His life, and died for me.

He came to shoulder my sin and
Paid a debt I could never pay
The sin weight of the world
Hung on his shoulders that glorious day.

[22]

Jesus is soon coming again
Lord, help me stay faithful ever abiding in your will
Your coming is filled with purpose
Your promises to fulfill.

Strength in Weakness

I am my strongest
With my knees bent and head bowed
Lord, I am not that clever
And surely, not that proud.

Seeking your truth and righteousness
On bended knees
Pleading for your love, forgiveness, and salvation
O, Lord hear and cleanse me please.

Cleanse my eyes to see your glory
As bright as can ever be
Brightly shining forevermore
Far, far into eternity.

Make my ears tender to hear
Your smallest whisper when you call my name
A voice that drowns, silences the world
Quiets all my fears, guilt, sin and shame.

Let the longing of my wretched soul
Hunger, thirst for only your presence can fill
Let me taste of your eternal goodness,
As I am covered in the center of your will.

So, Lord as I sojourn
Through this foreign land
Help me firmly plant my feet
Where you know I can stand.

I will abandon all pride and desires
No matter the cost
Touch my soul, heart
As I cling to and kneel at the foot of your Cross.

Because O' God, there, and only there
I will take my final rest
For all my trust and hope is
Rooted in your perfect Sacrifice that covers my sinfulness.

Those Moments

I wrestled with this moment
But never found the words to say
Many thoughts filled my mind
But did not fit this special day.

So, as I begin to think
On the goodness that God has done
These words began to flow
All one by one.

God has chosen His children
All from different walks of life
All felt the joy, the peace
All have seen the toils, the strife.

All have faced those moments
When they felt everything was lost
All realized the love and gain
Once they knelt at Calvary's Cross.

The blood from our dear Savior
Has covered mountains of sin
Has washed and cleansed us from without
and from deep within.

I pray that God continues to bless us
Wherever our feet may trod
To spread the life and love of Jesus
And the eternal riches of the Almighty God.

So, as we stand in His light
Looking up to God's only Son
Remember, Jesus is our victory
For the battle is already won.

About the Author

 The collection of poems in this book spans several years and reflect the experiences of Milton Bullard Jr. as he has walked down the trails of life. Milton viewed the various phases, places, and people he has encountered on these diverse paths through the lens of God, who continues to lead his way.

Milton was greatly inspired by his father. He treasures the many days of being on the fish banks with him in their hometown of Fort Pierce, Florida. His dad used those times as platforms to teach his young boys about God, the value of an education, personal integrity, and moral character. Though his dad had only a third-grade education, that did not hinder his ability to school his children on the trials and challenges they would face while travelling down the winding roads of life. More importantly, he explained to his boys how to react to these challenges. Yet, in all of this was the strength, prayers, and wisdom of my mother who guided the talents, drive, and mis-guided anger of her boys to be the productive individuals they have become today. Those quiet, meaningful moments culminated into some of the words expressed in these poems.

Milton is a service-connected veteran with many years of experience in the field of radiology. He finished an associate degree in radiologic science through George Washington University in Washington D.C. and then was awarded a bachelor's degree in healthcare management and leadership through National-Louis University in Chicago. Later, he obtained a second bachelor's degree in advanced radiologic studies from Weber State University in Ogden, Utah. After finishing his associate degree in theology, he went on to work as a Radiology Practitioner Assistant at a clinic in Jacksonville, Florida. Milton resides in Jacksonville Florida, with his lovely wife Andre. Together they have 4 adult children.

CPSIA information can be obtained
at www.ICGtesting.com
Printed in the USA
BVHW040940270721
613003BV00018B/800